PRESENTED TO:

_____

FROM:

_____

DATE:

_____

Because He Lives

*30 Blessings that Come
from His Life, Death,
and Resurrection*

ISBN 978-1-60587-559-0

Published by Freeman-Smith, a division of Worthy Media, Inc.,
134 Franklin Road, Suite 200, Brentwood, Tennessee 37027.

Scripture references marked KJV are from the Holy Bible, King James
Version

Scripture references marked NKJV are from the Holy Bible, New King
James Version. Copyright © 1982 by Thomas Nelson, Inc. Used by
permission.

Scripture references marked HCSB are from the Holman Christian
Standard Bible™ Copyright © 1999, 2000, 2001 by Holman Bible
Publishers. Used by permission.

Scripture references marked NIV are from the Holy Bible, New
International Version®. Copyright © 1973, 1978, 1984 International
Bible Society. Used by permission of Zondervan. All rights reserved.

Scripture references marked NASB are from the New American Standard
Bible®. Copyright © 1960, 1962, 1963, 1968, 1971, 1972, 1973, 1975, 1977,
1995 by The Lockman Foundation. Used by permission.

Cover Design by Thinkpendesign.com
Page Layout by Bart Dawson

Printed in the United States of America

1 2 3 4 5—CHG—17 16 15 14 13

Because He Lives

*30 Blessings that Come
from His Life, Death,
and Resurrection*

FREEMAN-SMITH

Table of Contents

Part I: For God So Loved the World   13

1. A Child Is Born   15
2. He Walked Among Us   23
3. The Treasures that Flow from His
    Servant Heart   29
4. A Priceless Gift: His Endless Love   35
5. He Does Not Change   41
6. Let Him Lead   47
7. God Gives Us Strength   51
8. The Joys of Church and Fellowship   57
9. Be Still   61
10. Liberated from Worry   65
11. The Power of Enthusiasm   69
12. Growing Every Day   73

Part II: A Cross and an Empty Tomb   77

13. Not My Will, but Thine   79
14. The Battle Has Been Won   85
15. Ultimate Security   89
16. The Empty Tomb   93
17. It Is Finished   99

Part III: Because He Lives   105

18. Because of the Cross, We Shall
    Also Live   107
19. Because He Lives, We Can Trust
    His Promises   113
20. Because of the Cross, Our Future
    Is Secure   117
21. Because He Lives, We Must Share
    the Good News   121
22. Because of the Cross, We Can
    Experience His Abundance   125
23. Ask Him   129
24. He Is Here   133
25. Your Purpose Begins at the Cross   137
26. Because He Lives, We Have Hope   141
27. The Ultimate Truth   145
28. Trusting God's Promises, Trusting
    God's Son   149
29. Honor Him   153
30. Because He Lives, We Can
    Celebrate Life   157

Now on the first day of the week,
very early in the morning, they,
and certain other women with them,
came to the tomb bringing the spices which
they had prepared. But they found the stone
rolled away from the tomb. Then they went
in and did not find the body of the Lord Jesus.
And it happened, as they were
greatly perplexed about this, that behold,
two men stood by them in shining garments.
Then, as they were afraid and bowed their
faces to the earth, they said to them,
"Why do you seek the living among the dead?
He is not here, but is risen!"

—

Luke 24:1-6 NKJV

Christ is risen! Hallelujah!
Gladness fills the world today;
From the tomb that
could not hold Him,
See, the stone is rolled away!

—

Fanny Crosby

PART I
FOR GOD
SO LOVED
THE WORLD

For God so loved the world,
that he gave his only begotten Son,
that whosoever believeth in him
should not perish, but have everlasting life.

—

John 3:16 KJV

He was the Son of God, but He wore a crown of thorns. He was the Savior of mankind, yet He was put to death on a roughhewn cross made of wood. He offered His healing touch to an unsaved world, and yet the same hands that had healed the sick and raised the dead were pierced with nails.

Jesus Christ, the Son of God, was born into humble circumstances. He walked this earth, not as a ruler of men, but as the Savior of mankind. His crucifixion, a torturous punishment that was intended to end His life and His reign, instead became the pivotal event in the history of all humanity.

Each year at Easter, we celebrate the death and resurrection of our Savior. Because Christ conquered death, we can conquer death. Because He lives, we can live eternally with Him. Because He was transformed, we can be transformed not just for today, but forever.

A CHILD IS BORN

*For unto you is born this day
in the city of David a Saviour,
which is Christ the Lord.*

—

Luke 2:11 KJV

Two thousand years ago, God sent His Son to transform the world and to save it. God's Son was born in the most humble of circumstances: in a nondescript village, to parents of simple means, far from the seats of earthly power.

And it came to pass in those days, that there went out a decree from Caesar Augustus, that all the world should be taxed . . . . And all went to be taxed, every one into his own city. And Joseph also went up from Galilee, out of the city of Nazareth, into Judea, unto the city of David, which is called Bethlehem, (because he was of the house and lineage of David) to be taxed with Mary his espoused wife, being great with child. And so it was, that, while they were there, the days were accomplished that she should be delivered. And she brought forth her firstborn son, and wrapped him in swaddling clothes, and laid him in a manger; because there was no room for them in the inn. And there were in the same country shepherds abiding in the field, keeping watch over their flock by night. And, lo, the angel of the Lord came upon them, and the glory of the Lord shone round about them; and they were sore afraid. And the angel said unto them, Fear not: for, behold, I bring you good tidings of great joy, which shall be to all people. For unto you is born this day in the city of David a Saviour, which is Christ the Lord. And this shall be a sign unto you; Ye shall find the babe wrapped in swaddling clothes, lying in a manger. And suddenly there was with the angel a multitude of the heavenly host praising God, and saying, Glory to God in the highest, and on earth peace, good will toward men.

Luke 2:1-14 KJV

The Christ child changed the world forever, and He can do the same for us. We, like shepherds tending our fields, are busy tending to the demands of daily life. But we must leave our duties behind, at least for a while, so that we may celebrate the One who has saved us. Let us celebrate Jesus: His birth, His life, His death, and His resurrection. Let us praise Him for His peace and His love. May we, like those shepherds of old, leave our fields—wherever they may be—and pause to worship God's priceless gift: His only begotten Son.

I have a great need for Christ;
I have a great Christ for my need.

C. H. Spurgeon

*In the beginning was the Word, and the Word
was with God, and the Word was God . . . .
And the Word was made flesh, and dwelt
among us, (and we beheld his glory,
the glory as of the only begotten of the Father,)
full of grace and truth.*

John 1:1, 14 KJV

To God be the glory,
great things He has done;
So loved He the world that
He gave us His Son.

Fanny Crosby

In every Christian, Christ lives again.
Every true believer is a return to
first-century Christianity.

Vance Havner

There is not a single thing that Jesus
cannot change, control, and conquer
because He is the living Lord.

Franklin Graham

The manger is a symbol of what can happen
when Jesus Christ resides inside us.

Bill Hybels

At the name of Jesus every knee should bow,
of things in heaven, and things in earth,
and things under the earth; and that every tongue
should confess that Jesus Christ is Lord,
to the glory of God the Father.

Philippians 2:10-11 KJV

Jesus said unto them,
Verily, verily, I say unto you,
Before Abraham was, I am.

—

John 8:58 KJV

A PRAYER

Dear Lord, keep me mindful of
Your priceless gift: my personal Savior,
Christ Jesus. Because He lives, I too will
live forever in heaven. Father, You loved
me before I was ever born, and You will
love me throughout eternity. In return,
let me offer my life to You so that
I might live according to Your
commandments and according to
Your plan. Let me always praise You,
Lord, as I give thanks for Your Son Jesus
and for Your everlasting love.

Amen

HE WALKED AMONG US

I have set you an example that
you should do as I have done for you.

—

John 13:15 NIV

Because Jesus walked among us, we are blessed now and throughout eternity. The blessings that come from His life, His death, and His resurrection are simply too numerous to count.

How marvelous it is that God became man. Had He not chosen to do so, we might feel removed from a distant Creator. But ours is not a distant God. Ours is a God who understands—far better than we ever could—the essence of what it means to be human.

God understands our hopes, our fears, and our temptations. He understands what it means to be angry and what it costs to forgive. He knows the heart, the conscience, and the soul of every person who has ever lived, including you. And God has a plan of salvation that is intended for you. Accept it. Accept God's gift through the person of His Son Christ Jesus.

God walked among us so that you might have eternal life; amazing though it may seem, He did it for all humanity, and He did it for you.

We say that Jesus preached the gospel,
but He did more. He came that there
might be a gospel to preach.

Oswald Chambers

Christ knows better than you
what it means to be human.

Joni Eareckson Tada

Christ's excellency is always fresh and new,
and it delights as much after it has
been seen for ten thousand years as when it
was seen the first moment.

Jonathan Edwards

Christians are not citizens of earth trying
to get to heaven, but citizens of heaven
making their way through this world.

Vance Havner

Tell me the story of Jesus.
Write on my heart every word.
Tell me the story most precious,
sweetest that ever was heard.

Fanny Crosby

Jesus—the standard of measurement,
the scale of weights, the test of character
for the whole moral universe.

R. G. Lee

Christ, the Son of God, the complete
embodiment of God's Word, came among us.
He looked on humanity's losing battle with
sin and pitched His divine tent in the middle
of the camp so that He could dwell among us.

Beth Moore

In His life, Christ is an example showing
us how to live; in His death,
He is a sacrifice satisfying for our sins.

Martin Luther

And surely I am with you always,
to the very end of the age.

Matthew 28:20 NIV

A PRAYER

Dear Lord, You sent Your Son to die on
a cross so that I might have eternal life.
And because Jesus was a man who walked
this earth, You possess a perfect
understanding of all humanity, including
my own frailties and shortcomings.
I praise You, Lord, for Your love,
for Your forgiveness, for Your grace,
and for Your Son. Let me share the
Good News of Jesus Christ, the One
who became a man so that I might
become His, not only for today,
but also for all eternity.
Amen

THE TREASURES THAT FLOW FROM HIS SERVANT HEART

But whosoever will be great among you, let him be your minister; and whosoever will be chief among you, let him be your servant: even as the Son of man came not to be ministered unto, but to minister, and to give his life a ransom for many.

—

Matthew 20:26-28 KJV

Because Jesus chose to serve, we are blessed. Because He was willing to sacrifice His life on the cross, we have the promise of eternal life and eternal love. And now, Christ calls upon each of us to become a servant, too.

Jesus taught that the most esteemed men and women are not the leaders of society or the politically powerful. To the contrary, Jesus taught that the greatest were those who chose to minister and to serve.

Today, you may feel the temptation to build yourself up in the eyes of your neighbors. Resist that temptation. Instead, serve your neighbors quietly and without fanfare. Find a need and fill it . . . humbly. Lend a helping hand and share a word of kindness . . . anonymously.

Today, take the time to minister to those in need. Then, when you have done your best to serve your neighbors and to serve your God, you can rest comfortably knowing that in the eyes of God you have achieved greatness. And

God's eyes, after all, are the only ones that really count.

Holy service in constant fellowship
with God is heaven below.

C. H. Spurgeon

Before the judgment seat of Christ,
my service will not be judged by how much
I have done but by how much
of me there is in it.

A. W. Tozer

Take my yoke upon you, and learn of me;
for I am meek and lowly in heart:
and ye shall find rest unto your souls.
For my yoke is easy, and my burden is light.

Matthew 11:29-30 KJV

Christianity, in its purest form, is nothing
more than seeing Jesus. Christian service,
in its purest form, is nothing more than
imitating Him who we see.
To see His Majesty and to imitate Him:
that is the sum of Christianity.

Max Lucado

You can judge how far you have risen in the
scale of life by asking one question:
How wisely and how deeply do I care?
To be Christianized is to be sensitized.
Christians are people who care.

E. Stanley Jones

No life can surpass that of a man who quietly
continues to serve God in the place where
providence has placed him.

C. H. Spurgeon

Giving to God and, in His name,
to others, is not something that we do;
it is the result of what we are.

Warren Wiersbe

Do all the good you can.
By all the means you can.
In all the ways you can.
In all the places you can.
At all the times you can.
To all the people you can.
As long as ever you can.

John Wesley

A PRAYER

Dear Lord, when Jesus humbled Himself
and became a servant, He also became
an example for His followers. Today,
as I serve my family and friends,
I do so in the name of Jesus, my Lord
and Master. Guide my steps, Father,
and let my service be pleasing to You.
Amen

A PRICELESS GIFT: HIS ENDLESS LOVE

Greater love has no one than this,
that he lay down his life for his friends.

—

John 15:13 NIV

Christ's life, death, and resurrection are all expressions of His love. Exactly how much does Jesus love us? More than we, as mere mortals, can comprehend. His love is perfect and steadfast. Even though we are fallible and wayward, the Good Shepherd cares for us still. Even though we have fallen far short of the Father's commandments, Christ loves us with a power and depth that are beyond our understanding. The sacrifice that Jesus made upon the cross was made for each of us, and His love endures to the edge of eternity and beyond.

Christ's love changes everything. When you accept His gift of grace, you are transformed, not only for today, but also for all eternity. If you haven't already done so, accept Jesus Christ as your Savior. He's waiting patiently for you to invite Him into your heart. Please don't make Him wait a single minute longer.

For while we were still helpless, at the appointed moment, Christ died for the ungodly.

Romans 5:6 HCSB

The love of God is one of the great realities of the universe, a pillar upon which the hope of the world rests. But it is a personal, intimate thing too. God does not love populations. He loves people. He loves not masses, but men.

A. W. Tozer

Almost 2,000 years ago, Jesus Christ won the decisive battle against sin and Satan through His death and resurrection. Satan did his best to defeat God's plans, but he could not win against God's overwhelming power.

Billy Graham

He loved us not because we're lovable,
but because He is love.

C. S. Lewis

The great love of God is an ocean
without a bottom or a shore.

C. H. Spurgeon

How do I love God? By doing beautifully
the work I have been given to do,
by doing simply that which God entrusted
to me, in whatever form it may take.

Mother Teresa

Christ is not valued at all unless
He is valued above all.

St. Augustine

Jesus Christ is the first and last,
author and finisher, beginning and end,
alpha and omega, and by Him all other things
hold together. He must be first or nothing.
God never comes next!

Vance Havner

God loves each of us
as if there were only one of us.

St. Augustine

For I am convinced that neither death, nor life,
nor angels, nor principalities, nor things present,
nor things to come, nor powers, nor height,
nor depth, nor any other created thing,
will be able to separate us from the love of God,
which is in Christ Jesus our Lord.

Romans 8:38-39 NASB

A PRAYER

Dear Jesus, I am humbled by Your love
and mercy. You went to Calvary so that
I might have eternal life. Thank You,
Jesus, for Your priceless gift, and
for Your love. You loved me first, Lord,
and I will return Your love
today and forever.
Amen

HE DOES NOT CHANGE

Jesus Christ is the same yesterday,
today, and forever.

—

Hebrews 13:8 HCSB

The challenges of everyday life are temporary, but the blessings that come from the cross are not. Those blessings, like God's love and protection, are eternal.

We live in a world that is always changing, but we worship a God who never changes—thank goodness. As believers, we can be comforted in the knowledge that our Heavenly Father is the rock that simply cannot be moved: "I am the Lord, I do not change" (Malachi 3:6 NKJV).

Are you facing difficult circumstances or unwelcome changes? If so, consider the cross. And, while you're at it, please remember that God is far bigger than any problem you may face. So, instead of worrying about life's inevitable obstacles, put your faith in the Father and His only begotten Son and rest assured: It is precisely because your Savior does not change that you can face your challenges with courage for this day and hope for the future.

The secret of contentment in the midst of
change is found in having roots in
the changeless Christ—the same
yesterday, today and forever.

Ed Young

The resurrection of Jesus Christ
is the power of God to change history
and to change lives.

Bill Bright

With God, it isn't who you were that matters;
it's who you are becoming.

Liz Curtis Higgs

God wants to revolutionize our lives—
by showing us how knowing Him
can be the most powerful force to help us
become all we want to be.

Bill Hybels

Christ's work of making new men
is not mere improvement,
but transformation.

C. S. Lewis

Believe and do what God says.
The life-changing consequences
will be limitless, and the results will be
confidence and peace of mind.

Franklin Graham

When the Spirit illuminates the heart,
then a part of the man sees which
never saw before; a part of him knows
which never knew before.

Oswald Chambers

When we become Christians,
we are not remodeled, nor are we
added to—we are transformed.

John MacArthur

If God can fashion the mountains, if God can
keep the sun in its orbit, if God can split
a sea and dry the ground beneath it so
an entire nation can cross, do you doubt that
He can transform your character?

Bill Hybels

A PRAYER

Dear Lord, our world changes, but You
are unchanging. When I face challenges
that leave me discouraged or fearful,
I will turn to You for strength and
assurance. Let my trust in You—
like Your love for me—
be unchanging and everlasting.
Amen

LET HIM LEAD

In all your ways acknowledge Him,
and He shall direct your paths.

—

Proverbs 3:6 NKJV

When we examine Christ's life, we learn how to live. When we consider Christ's death, we understand the price He paid for us. When we focus on Christ's love, we remind ourselves of the blessings that can be ours when we let Him guide our steps.

The Bible promises that God will guide you if you let Him. Your job, of course, is to let Him. But sometimes, you will be tempted to do otherwise. Sometimes, you'll be tempted to go along with the crowd; other times, you'll be tempted to do things your way, not God's way.

What will you allow to guide you through the coming day: your own desires (or, for that matter, the desires of your peers)? Or will you allow God's Son to lead the way? The answer should be obvious. You should let Jesus be your guide. When you entrust your life to Him completely and without reservation, He will give you the strength to meet any challenge, the courage to face any trial, and the wisdom to

live in His righteousness. So trust Christ today and seek His guidance. When you do, your
next step will most assuredly be the right one.

Fix your eyes upon the Lord!
Do it once. Do it daily. Do it constantly.
Look at the Lord and keep looking at Him.

Charles Swindoll

Good and evil both increase at compound
interest. That is why the little decisions
you and I make every day are of
such infinite importance.

C. S. Lewis

A PRAYER

Dear Lord, thank You for Your constant
presence and Your constant love.
I draw near to You this day with
the confidence that You are ready to
guide me. Help me walk closely with You,
Father, and help me share Your
Good News with all who cross my path.
Amen

GOD GIVES US STRENGTH

The name of the Lord is a strong tower;
The righteous run to it and are safe.

—

Proverbs 18:10 NKJV

It's a promise that is made over and over again in the Bible: Whatever "it" is, God can handle it.

Life isn't always easy. Far from it! Sometimes, life can seem like a long, tiring, character-building, fear-provoking journey. But even when the storm clouds form overhead, even during our darkest moments, we're protected by a loving Heavenly Father.

When we're worried, God can reassure us; when we're sad, God can comfort us. When our hearts are broken, God is not just near; He is here. So we must lift our thoughts and prayers to Him. When we do, He will answer our prayers. Why? Because He is our shepherd, and He has promised to protect us now and forever.

At the foot of the cross, we find protection and peace. Will you accept God's peace and wear God's armor against the frustrations and distractions of our dangerous world? If you do, you can live courageously and optimistically, knowing that even on the darkest days, you and your Heavenly Father can handle every challenge you face, today and forever.

The next time you're disappointed,
don't panic. Don't give up.
Just be patient and let God
remind you He's still in control.

Max Lucado

The promises of God's Word sustain us
in our suffering, and we know Jesus
sympathizes and empathizes
with us in our darkest hour.

Bill Bright

We do not understand the intricate pattern
of the stars in their course,
but we know that He Who created them does,
and that just as surely as He guides them,
He is charting a safe course for us.

Billy Graham

God's saints in all ages have realized
that God was enough for them.
God is enough for time;
God is enough for eternity.
God is enough!

—

Hannah Whitall Smith

A PRAYER

Dear Lord, You are my strength
and my shield. You rule over our world,
and I will allow You to rule over my heart.
I will obey Your commandments,
I will study Your Word, and I will seek
Your will for my life, today
and every day of my life.
Amen

THE JOYS OF CHURCH AND FELLOWSHIP

Worship the Lord with gladness.

Come before him, singing with joy.

Acknowledge that the Lord is God!

He made us, and we are his.

We are his people, the sheep of his pasture.

—

Psalm 100:2-3 NLT

Jesus loved His followers and He loved church. He understood that every church, no matter its size, can be a blessed place: a source of fellowship and strength.

If you want to build a better life, the church is a wonderful place to do it. Are you an active, contributing, member of your local fellowship? The answer to this simple question will have a profound impact on the direction of your spiritual journey and the content of your character.

If you are not currently engaged in a local church, you're missing out on an array of blessings that include, but are certainly not limited to, the life-lifting relationships that you can— and should—be experiencing with fellow believers.

So, find a congregation you're comfortable with, and join it. And once you've joined, don't just attend church out of habit. Go to church out of a sincere desire to know and worship God. When you do, you'll be blessed by the men and women who attend your fellowship, and you'll be blessed by your Creator. You deserve to attend church, and God deserves for you to attend church, so don't delay.

Only participation in the full life of
a local church builds spiritual muscle.

Rick Warren

Now you are the body of Christ,
and individual members of it.

1 Corinthians 12:27 HCSB

A PRAYER

Dear Lord, today I pray for Your church.
Let me help to feed Your flock by helping
to build Your church so that others, too,
might experience Your enduring love
and Your eternal grace.
Amen

BE STILL

Be still, and know that I am God....

—

Psalm 46:10 KJV

Are you so busy that you rush through the day with scarcely a single moment for quiet contemplation and prayer? If so, it's time to reorder your priorities.

We live in a noisy world, a world filled with distractions and complications. But if we allow them to separate us from God's peace, we do ourselves a profound disservice. If we are to maintain righteous minds and compassionate hearts, we must take time each day for prayer and for meditation. We must make ourselves still in the presence of our Creator. We must quiet our minds and our hearts so that we might sense God's will, God's love, and God's Son.

Has the busy pace of life robbed you of the peace that might otherwise be yours through Jesus Christ? Nothing is more important than the time you spend with your Savior. So be still and claim the inner peace that is your spiritual birthright: the peace of Jesus Christ. It is offered freely; it has been paid for in full; it is yours for the asking.

When we are in the presence of God,
removed from distractions, we are able to hear
Him more clearly, and a secure environment
has been established for the young and
broken places in our hearts to surface.

John Eldredge

Be still before the Lord
and wait patiently for him.

Psalm 37:7 NIV

Let your loneliness be transformed into
a holy aloneness. Sit still before the Lord.
Remember Naomi's word to Ruth:
"Sit still, my daughter, until you see
how the matter will fall."

Elisabeth Elliot

A PRAYER

Dear Lord, let me be still before You.
When I am hurried or distracted,
slow me down and redirect my thoughts.
When I am confused, give me perspective.
Keep me mindful, Father, that You are
always with me. And let me sense Your
presence today, tomorrow, and forever.

Amen

LIBERATED FROM WORRY

Don't worry about anything;
instead, pray about everything.
Tell God what you need,
and thank him for all he has done.

—

Philippians 4:6 NLT

Here's a riddle: What is it that is too unimportant to pray about yet too big for God to handle? The answer, of course, is: "nothing." Yet sometimes, when the challenges of the day seem overwhelming, we may spend more time worrying about our troubles than praying about them. And, we may spend more time fretting about our problems than solving them. A far better strategy is to pray as if everything depended entirely upon God and to work as if everything depended entirely upon us.

What we see as problems God sees as opportunities. And if we are to trust Him completely, we must acknowledge that even when our own vision is dreadfully impaired, His vision is perfect.

Let us trust God by courageously confronting the things that we see as problems and He sees as possibilities. And while we're at it, let's remind our friends and family members that no problem is too big for God.

God is bigger than your problems.
Whatever worries press upon you today,
put them in God's hands
and leave them there.

Billy Graham

Your heart must not be troubled.
Believe in God; believe also in Me.

John 14:1 HCSB

Today is mine. Tomorrow is none of my
business. If I peer anxiously into the fog
of the future, I will strain my spiritual eyes
so that I will not see clearly
what is required of me now.

Elisabeth Elliott

A PRAYER

Dear Lord, wherever I find myself,
let me celebrate more and worry less.
When my faith begins to waver, help me
to trust You more. Then, with praise on
my lips and the love of Your Son
in my heart, let me live courageously,
faithfully, prayerfully, and thankfully
this day and every day.
Amen

THE POWER OF ENTHUSIASM

Whatever you do, do it enthusiastically,
as something done for the Lord
and not for men.

—

Colossians 3:23 HCSB

Each day provides countless opportunities to serve God and to follow His Son. When we seize these opportunities with enthusiasm and excitement, we are blessed.

Are you enthused about your faith and your life, or do you struggle through each day giving scarcely a thought to God's blessings? And, are you excited about the possibilities for service that God has placed before you, whether at home, at work, or at church? You should be.

As you consider the magnitude of Christ's sacrifice and the enormity of His love, please remember that nothing is more important than your wholehearted commitment to God's only begotten Son. Your faith must never be an afterthought; it must be your ultimate priority, your ultimate possession, and your ultimate passion. When you become passionate about your faith, you'll become passionate about your life, too.

Norman Vincent Peale advised, "Get absolutely enthralled with something. Throw yourself into it with abandon. Get out of yourself. Be somebody. Do something." His words apply to you. So don't settle for a lukewarm existence. Instead, make the choice to become genuinely involved in life. The world needs your enthusiasm . . . and so do you.

Enthusiasm, like the flu, is contagious—
we get it from one another.

Barbara Johnson

Wouldn't it make an astounding difference,
not only in the quality of the work we do,
but also in the satisfaction, even our joy,
if we recognized God's gracious gift
in every single task?

Elisabeth Elliot

A PRAYER

Dear Lord, the Christian life is
a glorious adventure—let me share
my excitement with others. Let me be
an enthusiastic believer, Father,
and let me share my enthusiasm
today and every day.
Amen

GROWING EVERY DAY

*But grow in grace, and in the knowledge
of our Lord and Saviour Jesus Christ.
To him be glory both now and for ever.
Amen.*

—

2 Peter 3:18 KJV

The journey toward spiritual maturity lasts a lifetime: As Christians, we can and should continue to grow in the love and the knowledge of our Savior as long as we live. When we cease to grow, either emotionally or spiritually, we do ourselves and our loved ones a profound disservice. But, if we study God's Word, if we obey His commandments, and if we live in the center of His will, we will not be "stagnant" believers; we will, instead, be growing Christians . . . and that's exactly what God wants for our lives.

Many of life's most important lessons are painful to learn. During times of heartbreak and hardship, God stands ready to protect us. As Psalm 147 promises, "He heals the brokenhearted and bandages their wounds" (NCV). In His own time and according to His master plan, God will heal us if we invite Him into our hearts.

Spiritual growth need not take place only in times of adversity. We must seek to grow in our knowledge and love of the Lord every day that we live. In those quiet moments when we open our hearts to God, the One who made us keeps remaking us. He gives us direction, perspective, wisdom, and courage. The appropriate moment to accept those spiritual gifts is the present one.

Our Heavenly Father knows to
place us where we may learn lessons
impossible anywhere else.
He has neither misplaced
nor displaced us.

Elisabeth Elliot

A PRAYER

Heavenly Father, I want to grow closer
to You each day. I know that obedience
to Your will strengthens my relationship
with You, so help me to follow Your
commandments and obey Your Word
today . . . and every day of my life.
Amen

PART II
A CROSS AND AN EMPTY TOMB

Now upon the first day of the week,
very early in the morning, they came unto
the sepulchre, bringing the spices which
they had prepared, and certain others
with them. And they found the stone
rolled away from the sepulchre.
And they entered in, and found not
the body of the Lord Jesus.

—

Luke 24:1-3 KJV

The story of Easter is the story of an empty tomb. It is a story of betrayal, suffering, and death followed by resurrection, rejoicing, and eternal life. The story of Easter is God's message to the world that through Him we can—indeed we must—have hope. The story of Easter is the story of God's love, God's miracles, and God's offer of salvation.

Christ died so that we might have spiritual abundance, earthly peace, and eternal life. As we consider the empty tomb and all that it signifies, let us praise the Father and the Son for gifts that are too numerous to count, too profound to understand, and too costly to ever take for granted.

NOT MY WILL, BUT THINE

And he was withdrawn from them about a stone's cast, and kneeled down, and prayed, saying, Father, if thou be willing, remove this cup from me: nevertheless not my will, but thine, be done. And there appeared an angel unto him from heaven, strengthening him. And being in an agony he prayed more earnestly: and his sweat was as it were great drops of blood falling down to the ground.

—

Luke 22:41–44 KJV

When Jesus confronted the reality of His impending death on the cross, He asked God that this terrible burden might be lifted. But as He faced the possibility of a suffering that was beyond description, Jesus prayed, "Nevertheless not my will, but thine, be done" (Luke 22:42 KJV). As Christians, we too must be willing to accept God's will, even when we do not fully understand the reasons for the hardships that we must endure.

Grief and suffering visit all of us who live long and love deeply. When we lose a loved one, or when we experience any other profound loss, darkness overwhelms us for a while, and it seems as if we cannot summon the strength to face another day—but, with God's help, we can. When we confront circumstances that trouble us to the very core of our souls, we must trust God. When we are worried, we must turn our concerns over to Him. When we are anxious, we must be still and listen for the quiet assurance of God's promises. And then, by placing our lives in His hands, we learn that He is our shepherd today and throughout eternity. Let us trust the Shepherd.

The Almighty does nothing
without reason, although
the frail mind of man
cannot explain the reason.

St. Augustine

God does not give us everything we want,
but He does fulfill all His promises as
He leads us along the best and
straightest paths to Himself.

Dietrich Bonhoeffer

Trust in the LORD with all thine heart;
and lean not unto thine own understanding.
In all thy ways acknowledge him,
and he shall direct thy paths.

Proverbs 3:5-6 KJV

The God who orchestrates the universe
has a good many things to consider
that have not occurred to me, and it is well
that I leave them to Him.

Elisabeth Elliot

Your will should be corrected to
become identified with God's will.
You must not bend God's will to suit yours.

St. Augustine

The geography and the details of His plan
will be different for each one of us,
of course, but the Spirit's sovereign
working is far beyond what
the human mind can ever imagine.

Charles Swindoll

The only thing that can hinder us is our
own failure to work in harmony with
the plans of the Creator, and if this lack
of harmony can be removed,
then God can work.

Hannah Whitall Smith

A PRAYER

Dear Lord, let my faith be in You,
and in You alone. Without You, I am weak,
but when I trust You, I am protected.
In every aspect of my life, Father,
let me place my hope and my trust
in Your infinite wisdom and
Your boundless grace.
Amen

BLESSING 14

THE BATTLE HAS BEEN WON

But Jesus quickly spoke to them,
"Have courage! It is I. Do not be afraid."

—

Matthew 14:27 NCV

On that hill at Calvary, Jesus sacrificed Himself so that all Christians should have eternal life. If you have been touched by the transforming hand of God's Son, then you have every reason to be confident about your future here on earth and your future in heaven. But even if you are a faithful believer, you may find yourself discouraged by the inevitable setbacks and tragedies that are the inevitable price of life here on earth.

We Christians have many reasons to be confident. God is in His heaven; Christ has risen, and we are the sheep of His flock. Yet sometimes, even the most devout Christians can become discouraged. Discouragement, however, is not God's way; He is a God of possibility not negativity.

If your courage is being tested today, lean upon God's promises. Trust His Son. Remember that God is always near and that He is your protector and your deliverer. When you are worried, anxious, or afraid, call upon Him

and accept the touch of His comforting hand.
Remember that God rules both mountaintops
and valleys—with limitless wisdom and love—
now and forever.

Fill your mind with thoughts of God
rather than thoughts of fear.

Norman Vincent Peale

Seeing that a Pilot steers the ship in which
we sail, who will never allow us to perish
even in the midst of shipwrecks,
there is no reason why our minds
should be overwhelmed with fear and
overcome with weariness.

John Calvin

A PRAYER

Lord, sometimes, this world can be
a fearful place, but You have promised me
that You are with me always. Today, Lord,
I will live courageously as I place my trust
in Your everlasting power and my faith
in Your everlasting love.

Amen

ULTIMATE SECURITY

The Lord your God in your midst,
the Mighty One, will save; He will rejoice
over you with gladness, He will quiet
you with His love, He will rejoice
over you with singing.

—

Zephaniah 3:17 NKJV

When Christ died on the cross, He made that sacrifice for humanity and for you. Jesus is the best friend this world has ever known, and He is your ultimate source of security.

The world offers no safety nets, but God does. He sent His only begotten Son to offer you the priceless gift of eternal life. And now you are challenged to return God's love by obeying His commandments and honoring His Son.

When you allow Christ to reign over your life, you will be secure. When you and your beloved feel God's presence and invite His Son to rule your heart and your household, your family will be eternally blessed.

In a world filled with dangers and temptations, God is the ultimate armor. In a world filled with misleading messages, God's Word is the ultimate truth. In a world filled with more frustrations than we can count, God's Son offers the ultimate peace.

Will you accept God's peace and wear God's armor against the dangers of our world? Hopefully so—because when you do, you can live courageously, knowing that you possess the ultimate security: God's unfailing love for you.

In all the old castles of England, there was a place called the keep. It was always the strongest and best protected place in the castle, and in it were hidden all who were weak and helpless and unable to defend themselves in times of danger. Shall we be afraid to hide ourselves in the keeping power of our Divine Keeper, who neither slumbers nor sleeps, and who has promised to preserve our going out and our coming in, from this time forth and even forever more?

Hannah Whitall Smith

A PRAYER

Lord, let Your will be my will. When I am
confused, give me maturity and wisdom.
When I am worried, give me courage and
strength. Let me be Your faithful servant,
Father, always seeking Your guidance
and Your will for my life.

Amen

THE EMPTY TOMB

*But very early on Sunday morning the women
came to the tomb, taking the spices they had
prepared. They found that the stone covering
the entrance had been rolled aside. So they
went in, but they couldn't find the body of the
Lord Jesus. They were puzzled, trying to think
what could have happened to it. Suddenly,
two men appeared to them, clothed in dazzling
robes. The women were terrified and bowed
low before them. Then the men asked,
"Why are you looking in a tomb for
someone who is alive? He isn't here!
He has risen from the dead!"*

Luke 24:1-6 NLT

It was strict adherence to Jewish law that prevented Jesus' followers from returning to His tomb on the Sabbath day (the first day after His death). So it was not until Sunday morning that a small band of beleaguered Christians journeyed to the tomb in order to care for the body of their beloved teacher. But when they arrived, the tomb was empty. Jesus was gone. Angels proclaimed the glorious news: Jesus had risen from the dead.

Christ's resurrection is the cornerstone upon which the Christian faith is built. The resurrection gives hope and assurance to all of us who accept Jesus as our Lord and Savior. Because the Savior was raised from the dead, so too may we have the gift of eternal life if we believe in Him. The joy of the Easter message is as simple as it is profound: The tomb is empty. The Savoir lives. God's promise is fulfilled.

If only we would stop lamenting and look up,
God is here. Christ is risen. The Spirit
has been poured out from on high.

A. W. Tozer

A child of God should be
a visible beatitude for joy and a living
doxology for gratitude.

C. H. Spurgeon

The redemption, accomplished for us by our
Lord Jesus Christ on the cross at Calvary,
is redemption from the power of sin as well
as from its guilt. Christ is able to save all
who come unto God by Him.

Hannah Whitall Smith

Blessed be the God and Father of our Lord Jesus Christ, who according to His great mercy has caused us to be born again to a living hope through the resurrection of Jesus Christ from the dead.

1 Peter 1:3 NASB

Let us see the victorious Jesus, the conqueror of the tomb, the one who defied death. And let us be reminded that we, too, will be granted the same victory.

Max Lucado

The way to be saved is not to delay, but to come and take.

D. L. Moody

There is no one so far lost that Jesus cannot
find him and cannot save him.

Andrew Murray

The work of Jesus is the creation of saints.

Oswald Chambers

I now know the power of the risen Lord!
He lives! The dawn of Easter has broken
in my own soul! My night is gone!

Mrs. Charles E. Cowman

The Gospel is not so much a demand
as it is an offer, an offer of new life
to man by the grace of God.

E. Stanley Jones

A PRAYER

Lord, You have saved me by Your grace.
Keep me mindful that Your grace is a gift
that I can accept but cannot earn.
I praise You for that priceless gift, today
and forever. Let me share the good news
of Your grace with a world that
desperately needs Your healing touch.
Amen

IT IS FINISHED

After this, Jesus, knowing that all things had already been accomplished, to fulfill the Scripture, said, "I am thirsty." A jar full of sour wine was standing there; so they put a sponge full of the sour wine upon a branch of hyssop and brought it up to His mouth. Therefore when Jesus had received the sour wine, He said, "It is finished!" And He bowed His head and gave up His spirit.

—

John 19:28–30 NASB

On a Friday morning, on a hill at Calvary, Jesus was crucified. Darkness came over the land, the curtain of the temple was torn in two, and finally Jesus called out, "Father, into your hands I commit my spirit" (Luke 23:46 NIV). Christ had endured the crucifixion, and now it was finished.

The body of Jesus was wrapped in a linen shroud and placed in a new tomb. It was there that God breathed life into His Son. It was there that Christ was resurrected. It was there that the angels rejoiced. And it was there, that God's plan for the salvation of mankind was to be made complete.

Christ proved His love for you and me on the cross at Calvary. His love is perfect and unchanging; it does not waver, and it does not pass away. In return, we are called to be steadfast in our love for Him.

As we accept Christ's love and honor His commandments, our lives bear testimony to His power and to His grace. Christ's love changes everything. May we accept it and share it, to-day, tomorrow, and forever.

In the wounds of the dying Savior,
see the love of the great I AM.

C. H. Spurgeon

The spectacle of the Cross, the most public
event of Jesus' life, reveals the vast
difference between a god who proves
himself through power and One who proves
himself through love.

Philip Yancey

Costly grace is the treasure hidden in
the field; for the sake of it, a man will gladly
go and sell all that He has. It is costly
because it costs a man his life, and it is grace
because it gives a man the only true life.

Dietrich Bonhoeffer

Grace: a gift that costs everything for
the giver and nothing for the recipient.

Philip Yancey

There is no greater joy than the peace and
assurance of knowing that, whatever
the future may hold, you are secure
in the loving arms of the Savior.

Billy Graham

The grace of God is sufficient for all
our needs, for every problem, and for every
difficulty, for every broken heart,
and for every human sorrow.

Peter Marshall

The grace of God is infinite and eternal.
As it had no beginning, so it can have no end,
and being an attribute of God,
it is as boundless as infinitude.

A. W. Tozer

God proved His love on the cross. When
Christ hung, and bled, and died it was God
saying to the world—I love you.

Billy Graham

A PRAYER

Dear Jesus, You gave Your life for me.
Your love is boundless, infinite,
and eternal. Today, let me pause
and reflect upon Your sacrifice,
Your gift of grace, and Your love.
Amen

PART III
BECAUSE HE LIVES

If we have died with Christ,
we believe that we shall
also live with Him

—

Romans 6:8 NASB

Christ endured the crown of thorns and the cross at Golgotha so that we might have the gift of eternal life. Now, each of us must claim that gift as our own.

Let us accept the Savior into our hearts. Let us share His Good News. Let us obey His commandments. Let us accept His abundance and His peace.

Let us pick up His cross and follow Him wherever He may lead. Let us trust Him with our lives, our hearts, and our souls, this day and forever.

BECAUSE OF THE CROSS, WE SHALL ALSO LIVE

Truly, truly, I say to you, he who hears My word, and believes Him who sent Me, has eternal life, and does not come into judgment, but has passed out of death into life. Truly, truly, I say to you, an hour is coming and now is, when the dead will hear the voice of the Son of God, and those who hear will live.

—

John 5:24–25 NASB

Christ sacrificed His life on the cross so that we might have life eternal. This gift, freely given from God's only begotten Son, is the priceless possession of everyone who accepts Him as Lord and Savior. Thankfully, grace is not an earthly reward for righteous behavior; it is, instead, a blessed spiritual gift. When we accept Christ into our hearts, we are saved by His grace.

The familiar words from the book of Ephesians make God's promise perfectly clear: "For it is by grace you have been saved, through faith—and this not from yourselves, it is the gift of God—not by works, so that no one can boast" (2:8-9 NIV).

God's grace is the ultimate gift, and we owe to Him the ultimate in thanksgiving. Let us praise the Creator for His priceless gift, and let us share the Good News with the world. We return our Father's love by accepting His grace and by sharing His message and His love. When we do, we are eternally blessed. God is waiting patiently for each of us to accept His gift of eternal life. Let us claim Christ's gift today.

The seed of God stirred, shoved, and sprouted.
The ground trembled, and the rock
of the tomb tumbled.
And the flower of Easter blossomed.

Max Lucado

The crucial question for each of us is this:
What do you think of Jesus, and do you yet
have a personal acquaintance with Him?

Hannah Whitall Smith

Jesus is the personal approach from the
unseen God coming so near that He becomes
inescapable. You don't have to find Him—
you just have to consent to be found.

E. Stanley Jones

When we invite Jesus into our lives,
we experience life in the fullest,
most vital sense.

Catherine Marshall

And because we know Christ is alive,
we have hope for the present and hope
for life beyond the grave.

Billy Graham

God's goal is not to make you happy.
It is to make you His.

Max Lucado

Once grace has scrubbed the soul,
anyone can take their place in
the lineage of the Son of God.

Calvin Miller

If we only believe and ask,
a full measure of God's grace is
available to any of us.

Charles Swindoll

No one is beyond His grace.
No situation, anywhere on earth,
is too hard for God.

Jim Cymbala

Thanks be to God for his indescribable gift!
2 Corinthians 9:15 NIV

A PRAYER

Lord, I am only here on this earth for
a brief while. But, You have offered me
the priceless gift of eternal life through
Your Son Jesus. I accept Your gift, Lord,
with thanksgiving and praise. Let me share
the good news of my salvation with
those who need Your healing touch.
Amen

BECAUSE HE LIVES, WE CAN TRUST HIS PROMISES

Therefore whosoever heareth these sayings of mine, and doeth them, I will liken him unto a wise man, which built his house upon a rock: and the rain descended, and the floods came, and the winds blew, and beat upon that house; and it fell not: for it was founded upon a rock.

—

Matthew 7:24-25 KJV

God's Holy Word is a unique blessing and a priceless treasure. The words of Matthew 4:4 remind us that, "Man shall not live by bread alone but by every word that proceedeth out of the mouth of God" (KJV). As believers, we must study the Bible and meditate upon its meaning for our lives. Otherwise, we deprive ourselves of a priceless gift from our Creator.

God's Word is unlike any other book. The Bible is a roadmap for life here on earth and for life eternal. As Christians, we are called upon to study God's Holy Word, to follow its commandments, and to share its Good News with the world.

Jonathan Edwards advised, "Be assiduous in reading the Holy Scriptures. This is the fountain whence all knowledge in divinity must be derived. Therefore let not this treasure lie by you neglected." God's Holy Word is, indeed, His timeless guide to life here on earth and life eternal. A passing acquaintance with the Good

Book is insufficient for Christians who seek to obey God's Word and to understand His will. After all, man does not live by bread alone . . .

Faith expects from God
what is beyond all expectation.

Andrew Murray

If we have the true love of God in our hearts,
we will show it in our lives.
We will not have to go up and down
the earth proclaiming it.
We will show it in everything we say or do.

D. L. Moody

A PRAYER

Lord, direct my path far from
the temptations and distractions of
the world. Make me a worthy example
to my family and friends. And, let my
kind words and my good deeds serve as
a testimony to the changes You have
made in my life. Let me praise You, Father,
by following in the footsteps of Your Son,
and let others see Him through me.

Amen

BECAUSE OF THE CROSS, OUR FUTURE IS SECURE

❁

Do not let your hearts be troubled.

Trust in God; trust also in me.

In my Father's house are many rooms;

if it were not so, I would have told you.

I am going there to prepare a place for you.

—

John 14:1-2 NIV

Sometimes the future seems bright, and sometimes it does not. Yet even when we cannot see the possibilities of tomorrow, God can. As believers, our challenge is to trust an uncertain future to an all-powerful God.

Christ's life, death, and resurrection form the cornerstone of the Christian faith. Jesus rose from the dead, and through Him we, too, can have eternal life. Christ's sacrifice is the ultimate blessing, and we should trust Him always.

When we trust God, we should trust Him without reservation. We should steel ourselves against the inevitable disappointments of the day, secure in the knowledge that our Heavenly Father has a plan for the future that only He can see.

Can you place your future into the hands of a loving and all-knowing God? Can you live amid the uncertainties of today, knowing that God has dominion over all your tomorrows?

If you can, you are wise and you are blessed.
When you trust God with everything you are
and everything you have, He will bless you
now and forever.

You can look forward with hope, because one
day there will be no more separation, no more
scars, and no more suffering in My Father's
House. It's the home of your dreams!

Anne Graham Lotz

The future lies all before us.
Shall it only be a slight advance upon what
we usually do? Ought it not to be a bound,
a leap forward to altitudes of endeavor and
success undreamed of before?

Annie Armstrong

A PRAYER

Dear Lord, as I look to the future,
I will place my trust in You. If I become
discouraged, I will turn to You.
If I am afraid, I will seek strength in You.
You are my Father, and I will place my hope,
my trust, and my faith in You.

Amen

BECAUSE HE LIVES, WE MUST SHARE THE GOOD NEWS

Now then we are ambassadors

for Christ . . . .

—

2 Corinthians 5:20 KJV

After His resurrection, Jesus addressed His disciples:

> But the eleven disciples proceeded to Galilee, to the mountain which Jesus had designated. When they saw Him, they worshiped Him; but some were doubtful. And Jesus came up and spoke to them, saying, "All authority has been given to Me in heaven and on earth. Go therefore and make disciples of all the nations, baptizing them in the name of the Father and the Son and the Holy Spirit, teaching them to observe all that I commanded you; and lo, I am with you always, even to the end of the age."
>
> Matthew 28:16–20 NASB

Christ's great commission applies to Christians of every generation, including our own. As believers, we are called to share the Good News of Jesus Christ with our families, with our neighbors, and with the world. Jesus commanded His disciples to become fishers of men. We must do likewise, and we must do so today. Tomorrow may indeed be too late.

God is not saving the world; it is done.
Our business is to get men
and women to realize it.

Oswald Chambers

Christ is our temple,
in whom by faith all believers meet.

Matthew Henry

A PRAYER

Heavenly Father, every man and
woman, every boy and girl is Your child.
You desire that all Your children know
Jesus as their Lord and Savior. Father,
let me be part of Your Great Commission.
Let me give, let me pray, and let me
go out into this world so that I might be
a fisher of men . . . for You.

Amen

BECAUSE OF THE CROSS, WE CAN EXPERIENCE HIS ABUNDANCE

I have come that they may have life,
and that they may have it
more abundantly.

—

John 10:10 NKJV

The familiar words of John 10:10 should serve as a daily reminder: Christ came to this earth so that we might experience His abundance, His love, and His gift of eternal life. But Christ does not force Himself upon us; we must claim His gifts for ourselves.

Sometimes, when we're busy or hurried, abundance seems a distant promise. It is not. Every day, we can claim the spiritual abundance that God promises for our lives . . . and we should.

Thomas Brooks spoke for believers of every generation when he observed, "Christ is the sun, and all the watches of our lives should be set by the dial of His motion." Christ, indeed, is the ultimate Savior of mankind and the personal Savior of those who believe in Him. As His servants, we should place Him at the very center of our lives. And, every day that God gives us breath, we should share Christ's love and His abundance with a world that needs both.

The gift of God is eternal life, spiritual life,
abundant life through faith in Jesus Christ,
the Living Word of God.

Anne Graham Lotz

God loves you and wants you to experience
peace and life—abundant and eternal.

Billy Graham

The Bible says that being a Christian
is not only a great way to die,
but it's also the best way to live.

Bill Hybels

The story of every great Christian
achievement is the history of answered prayer.

E. M. Bounds

A PRAYER

Heavenly Father, You have promised
an abundant life through Your Son Jesus.
Thank You, Lord, for Your abundance.
Guide me according to Your will, so that
I might be a worthy servant in all that
I say and do, this day and every day.

Amen

ASK HIM

*The earnest prayer of a righteous person
has great power and wonderful results.*

—

James 5:16 NLT

Prayer is a blessing, a precious gift from above. So, Jesus made it clear to His disciples that they should petition God for the things they needed. So should we. Genuine, heartfelt prayer produces powerful changes in us and in our world. When we lift our hearts to God, we open ourselves to a never-ending source of divine wisdom and infinite love.

James 5:16 makes a promise that God intends to keep: when you pray earnestly, fervently, and often, great things will happen. Too many people, however, are too timid or too pessimistic to ask God to do big things. Please don't count yourself among their number.

God has promised that when you ask for His help, He will not withhold it. So ask. Ask Him to meet the needs of your day. Ask Him to lead you, to protect you, and to correct you. Then, trust the answers He gives.

God stands at the door and waits. When you knock, He opens. When you ask, He answers. Your task, of course, is to seek His guidance prayerfully, confidently, and often.

Don't be afraid to ask your Heavenly Father
for anything you need. Indeed, nothing
is too small for God's attention or
too great for His power.

Dennis Swanberg

God will help us become the people we are
meant to be, if only we will ask Him.

Hannah Whitall Smith

We honor God by asking for great things
when they are a part of His promise.
We dishonor Him and cheat ourselves when
we ask for molehills where
He has promised mountains.

Vance Havner

A PRAYER

Dear Lord, I will open my heart to You.
I will take my concerns, my fears,
my plans, and my hopes to You in prayer.
And, then, I will trust the answers that
You give. You are my loving Father,
and I will accept Your will for my life
today and every day that I live.
Amen

BLESSING 24

HE IS HERE

❦

The eyes of the Lord are everywhere,
keeping watch on
the wicked and the good.

—

Proverbs 15:3 NIV

In the quiet early morning, as the sun's first rays peak over the horizon, we may sense the presence of God. But as the day wears on and the demands of everyday life bear down upon us, we may become so wrapped up in earthly concerns that we forget to praise the Creator.

God is everywhere we have ever been and everywhere we will ever be. When we turn to Him often, we are blessed by His presence. But, if we ignore God's presence or rebel against it altogether, the world in which we live soon becomes a spiritual wasteland.

Since God is everywhere, we are free to sense His presence whenever we take the time to quiet our souls and turn our prayers to Him. But sometimes, amid the incessant demands of everyday life, we turn our thoughts far from God; when we do, we suffer.

Are you tired, discouraged, or fearful? Be comforted because God is with you. Are you confused? Listen to the quiet voice of your

Heavenly Father. Are you bitter? Talk with God and seek His guidance. Are you celebrating a great victory? Thank God and praise Him. He is the Giver of all things good. In whatever condition you find yourself—whether you are happy or sad, victorious or vanquished, troubled or triumphant—celebrate God's presence. And be comforted in the knowledge that God is not just near. He is here.

The next time you hear a baby laugh
or see an ocean wave, take note.
Pause and listen as His Majesty
whispers ever so gently, "I'm here."

Max Lucado

A PRAYER

Dear Lord, You are with me always.
Help me feel Your presence in every
situation and every circumstance.
Today, Dear God, let me feel You and
acknowledge Your presence,
Your love, and Your Son.
Amen

YOUR PURPOSE BEGINS AT THE CROSS

You make known to me the path of life;
you will fill me with joy in your presence,
with eternal pleasures at your right hand.

—

Psalm 16:11 NIV

God has things He wants you to do and places He wants you to go. The most important decision of your life is, of course, your commitment to accept Jesus Christ as your personal Lord and Savior. And, once your eternal destiny is secured, you will undoubtedly ask yourself the question "What now, Lord?" If you earnestly seek God's will for your life, you will find it . . . in time.

As you prayerfully consider God's path for your life, you should study His Word and be ever watchful for His signs. You should associate with fellow believers who will encourage your spiritual growth, and you should listen to that inner voice that speaks to you in the quiet moments of your daily devotionals.

As you continually seek God's purpose for your life, be patient: your Heavenly Father may not always reveal Himself as quickly as you would like. But rest assured: God is here, and He intends to use you in wonderful, unexpected ways. He desires to lead you along a path

of His choosing as a means to honor His Son
and share His Good News. Your challenge is to
watch, to listen . . . and to follow.

For it is God who is working among you
both the willing and the working for
His good purpose.
Philippians 2:13 HCSB

When God speaks to you through the Bible,
prayer, circumstances, the church,
or in some other way,
He has a purpose in mind for your life.
Henry Blackaby and Claude King

A PRAYER

Dear Lord, I know that You have
a purpose for my life, and I will seek
that purpose today and every day
that I live. Let my actions be pleasing
to You, and let me share Your Good News
with a world that so desperately
needs Your healing hand and
the salvation of Your Son.
Amen

BECAUSE HE LIVES, WE HAVE HOPE

For I know the thoughts that I think toward you, says the Lord, thoughts of peace and not of evil, to give you a future and a hope. Then you will call upon Me and go and pray to Me, and I will listen to you.

—

Jeremiah 29:11-12 NKJV

ecause Jesus conquered death, we have hope. Yet, sometimes, hope can be a highly perishable commodity. When the challenges and pressures of everyday life threaten to overwhelm us, we may convince ourselves that the future holds little promise—and we may allow our fears to eclipse our dreams.

The hope that the world offers is fleeting and imperfect. The hope that God offers is unchanging, unshakable, and unending. It is no wonder, then, that when we seek security from worldly sources, our hopes are often dashed. Thankfully, God has no such record of failure.

Where will you place your hopes today? Will you entrust your future to man or to the Son of God? Will you seek solace exclusively from fallible human beings, or will you place your hopes, first and foremost, in the trusting hands of your Creator?

Today, as you embark upon the next stage of your life's journey, consider the words of the

Psalmist: "You are my hope; O Lord GOD, You are my confidence" (71:5 NASB). Then, place your trust in the One who cannot be shaken.

I discovered that sorrow was not to
be feared but rather endured with hope
and expectancy that God would use it
to visit and bless my life.

Jill Briscoe

Never yield to gloomy anticipation.
Place your hope and confidence in God.
He has no record of failure.

Mrs. Charles E. Cowman

A PRAYER

Dear Lord, You are my sovereign God.
Your Son defeated death; He overcame
the world; He gives me life abundant.
Your Holy Spirit comforts and guides me.
Let me celebrate all Your gifts,
and make me a hope-filled Christian
today and every day that I live.
Amen

THE ULTIMATE TRUTH

For everyone who practices wicked things hates the light and avoids it, so that his deeds may not be exposed. But anyone who lives by the truth comes to the light, so that his works may be shown to be accomplished by God.

—

John 3:20–21 HCSB

The life, death, and resurrection are inescapable truths that have shaped human history and will reshape eternity. The familiar words of John 8:32 remind us that "you shall know the truth, and the truth shall make you free" (NKJV). And St. Augustine had this advice: "Let everything perish! Dismiss these empty vanities! And let us take up the search for the truth."

God is vitally concerned with truth. His Word teaches the truth; His Spirit reveals the truth; His Son leads us to the truth. When we open our hearts to God, and when we allow His Son to rule over our thoughts and our lives, God reveals Himself, and we come to understand the truth about ourselves and the Truth about God's gift of grace.

Are you seeking God's truth and making decisions in light of that truth? Hopefully so. When you do, you'll discover that the truth will indeed set you free, now and forever.

However, when He, the Spirit of truth,
has come, He will guide you into all truth.

John 16:13 NKJV

The faith and love that spring from the hope
stored up for you in heaven and about which you
have already heard in the true message of the
gospel that has come to you. In the same way,
the gospel is bearing fruit and growing throughout
the whole world—just as it has been doing among
you since the day you heard it
and truly understood God's grace.

Colossians 1:5-6 NIV

We have in Jesus Christ a perfect example of
how to put God's truth into practice.

Bill Bright

A PRAYER

Heavenly Father, let me trust in
Your Word and in Your Son. Jesus said
He was the truth, and I believe Him.
Make Jesus the standard for truth in
my life so that I might be
a worthy example to others and
a worthy servant to You.
Amen

TRUSTING GOD'S PROMISES, TRUSTING GOD'S SON

Heaven and earth will pass away,
but my words will never pass away.

—

Matthew 24:35 NIV

For thoughtful believers, every day begins and ends with God's Son and God's promises. When we accept Christ into our hearts, God promises us the opportunity for earthly peace and spiritual abundance. But more importantly, God promises us the priceless gift of eternal life.

Are you standing on the promises of God? Are you expecting Him to do wonderful things, or are you living beneath a cloud of apprehension and doubt? The familiar words of Psalm 118:24 remind us of a profound yet simple truth: "This is the day which the LORD hath made; we will rejoice and be glad in it" (KJV). Do you trust that promise, and do you live accordingly? If so, you are living the passionate life that God intends.

As we face the inevitable challenges of life-here-on-earth, we must arm ourselves with the promises of God's Holy Word. When we do, we can expect the best, not only for the day ahead, but also for all eternity.

God has made promises to mankind and to you. God's promises never fail and they never grow old. You must trust those promises and share them with your family, with your friends, and with the world.

Faith is the virtue that enables us
to believe and obey the Word of God,
for faith comes from hearing and hearing
from the Word of God.

Franklin Graham

The stars may fall, but God's promises
will stand and be fulfilled.

J. I. Packer

A PRAYER

Lord, Your Holy Word contains promises,
and I will trust them. I will use
the Bible as my guide, and I will trust You,
Lord, to speak to me through Your
Holy Spirit and through Your Holy Word,
this day and forever.
Amen

BLESSING 29

HONOR HIM

The LORD is my strength and song,
and He has become my salvation;
He is my God, and I will praise Him.

—

Exodus 15:2 NIV

As we consider Christ's sacrifice on the cross and His resurrection, we are humbled by His love. And because we owe Christ so much, we must praise Him with our prayers, our words, and our deeds.

Mrs. Charles E. Cowman, the author of the classic devotional text *Streams in the Desert*, wrote, "Two wings are necessary to lift our souls toward God: prayer and praise. Prayer asks. Praise accepts the answer." Today, as you hug your child or kiss your spouse, or as you gaze upon a passing cloud or marvel at a glorious sunset, think of what God has done for you and for yours. And, every time you notice a gift from the Giver of all things good, praise Him. His works are marvelous, His gifts are beyond understanding, and His love endures forever.

Make a joyful noise unto the LORD,
all ye lands. Serve the LORD with gladness:
come before his presence with singing.

Psalm 100:1-2 KJV

No part of our prayers creates
a greater feeling of joy than when we praise
God for who He is. He is our Master Creator,
our Father, our source of all love.

Shirley Dobson

The LORD is my strength and song,
and He has become my salvation;
He is my God, and I will praise Him.

Exodus 15:2 NIV

This is my story, this is my song,
praising my Savior, all the day long.

Fanny Crosby

A PRAYER

Heavenly Father, Your gifts are greater
than I can imagine, and Your love for me
is greater than I can fathom. May I live
each day with thanksgiving in my heart
and praise on my lips. Thank You for
the gift of Your Son and for the promise
of eternal life. Let me share the joyous
news of Jesus Christ with a world
that needs His healing touch
this day and every day.
Amen

BECAUSE HE LIVES, WE CAN CELEBRATE LIFE

The stone the builders rejected has become the capstone; the LORD has done this, and it is marvelous in our eyes. This is the day the LORD has made; let us rejoice and be glad in it.

—

Psalm 118:22-24 NIV

Every day is a good day to celebrate God's blessings. And every day is a good day to give thanks to His Son.

The 118th Psalm reminds us that today is, indeed, a cause for celebration. God gives us this day; He fills it to the brim with possibilities, and He challenges us to use it for His purposes. The day is presented to us fresh and clean at midnight, free of charge, but we must beware: Today is a non-renewable resource— once it's gone, it's gone forever. Our responsibility, of course, is to use this day in the service of God's will and according to His commandments.

Today, give thanks for Christ and treasure the time that God has given you. Give the Father the glory, the praise, and the thanksgiving that He deserves. And search for the hidden possibilities that God has placed along your path. This day is a priceless gift from God, so use it joyfully and encourage others to do likewise.

God is the giver, and we are the receivers.
And His richest gifts are bestowed
not upon those who do the greatest things,
but upon those who accept
His abundance and His grace.

Hannah Whitall Smith

The Lord is glad to open the gate to
every knocking soul. It opens very freely;
its hinges are not rusted; no bolts secure it.
Have faith and enter at this moment through
holy courage. If you knock with a heavy heart,
you shall yet sing with joy of spirit.
Never be discouraged!

C. H. Spurgeon

When Jesus Christ is the source of our joy,
no words can describe it.

Billy Graham

A PRAYER

Dear Lord, You have given me
so many reasons to celebrate. Today,
let me choose an attitude of cheerfulness.
Let me be a joyful Christian, Lord, quick
to laugh and slow to anger. And, let me
share Your goodness with my family,
my friends, and my neighbors,
this day and every day.
Amen